ECCENTRIC PLANET
A Play

JOHN BARROW

Copyright © 2013 John Barrow
All rights reserved.
ISBN: 061581591X
ISBN 13: 9780615815916
Library of Congress Control Number: 2013909390
Wheelbarrow Books New York, NY

ECCENTRIC PLANET

Characters:

GEORG JOACHIM RHETICUS, *late twenties*
NICOLAS COPERNICUS, *late sixties*
PHILIPP MELANCHTHON, *early forties*
TIEDEMANN GIESE, *early sixties*
JOHANNES DANTISCUS, *late fifties*
ANNA SCHILLING, *early forties*
KARL, *early twenties*
Apart from Karl, the characters in this play were historical persons.

Time: 1539-1543

Place: Frauenberg: Cathedral compound
Wittenberg: Melanchthon's study
Löbau Castle: Bishop Giese's quarters
Danzig: Anna's residence

Scene One

Lights reveal COPERNICUS *in his study in Frauenberg.* GIESE *enters. The year is 1539.*

GIESE: Bishop Dantiscus has given his final answer. There will be no further negotiations. The woman has to go.

COPERNICUS: Then that settles it.

GIESE: I never understood why you brought her here in the first place.

COPERNICUS: She was a great help. She kept the place clean; she darned my socks.

GIESE: You could have had someone come in daily. There must have been more to it.

COPERNICUS: There was. I thought we might have children.

GIESE: Really? Why didn't you?

COPERNICUS: It never happened. After a few years I stopped trying. It seems a foolish notion now—an old churchman wanting a family. But I had seen my life dry up before my eyes. I thought a son or daughter would give me something, a place in the chain of life.

GIESE: Not everyone was meant to have children. You have a special calling. You are a scientist.

COPERNICUS: Anna was with me for eight years. I feel I've betrayed her.

GIESE: She chose to stay with you.

COPERNICUS: And has nothing to show for it. Poor Anna. She was furious with me, furious with the bishop—he makes no secret of his children—

GIESE: They were born before he entered the church.

COPERNICUS: She thinks I should have fought him. But you don't fight a bishop.

KARL enters.

KARL: A letter for you, sir.

COPERNICUS: Thank you, Karl.

GIESE: This is little Karl? I haven't seen you since you were this high. *(He raises hand to indicate lower height.)*

KARL: I've grown up, Your Excellency.

COPERNICUS: That will be all, Karl. *(KARL exits.)*

Light reveals RHETICUS at right, writing letter. He wears plain clothing.

COPERNICUS *(perusing letter):* The Lutheran has written me another letter.

GIESE: He certainly is persistent. I should think you'd be flattered.

COPERNICUS: I'm not flattered.

Lights dim on COPERNICUS *and* GIESE.

RHETICUS *(writing letter):* My most revered and illustrious Dr. Copernicus, I present myself humbly, and in deep admiration of your work, which—if the rumors are true—may be compared to the labors of Hercules or even to the exquisite devices of Apollo. I am Georg Joachim Rheticus, aged twenty-five, professor of mathematics and astronomy at the University of Wittenberg. I long to find men of great knowledge and learn from their experience. This quest has taken me to diverse points of Germany, seeking the teacher who can best instruct me. In this, I follow that charming sentiment of the ancient Greeks, who said: "The opinions of older men are better." What a wonderful age we live in! The arts are blessed with genius, the sciences flourish, a new world has been found in the west, and new possibilities stretch to an endless horizon. It is rumored that you have discovered the true nature of the universe. As we men of science are servants of Truth, I most fervently wish to present myself as your student. With utmost regard and humble entreaties, et cetera, et cetera.

Lights on COPERNICUS *and* GIESE.

COPERNICUS *(still reading letter):* He says he'll arrive sometime next month.

GIESE: It's a good thing. He'll take your mind off this business with the bishop. A student might be a welcome distraction.

COPERNICUS: Absolutely not. I will not have a student.

GIESE: I'm sorry I won't be here when he arrives. I'd love to see the sparks fly.

COPERNICUS: There won't be sparks. I just wish you didn't have to return to Löbau. I dread telling Anna.

GIESE: Bishop Dantiscus has spoken.

COPERNICUS: And I must obey.

GIESE: I'm sorry you've had to endure this.

COPERNICUS: It'll pass. But the loneliness is starting to wear on me. I would give anything to have a kindred spirit to talk to on these long evenings.

GIESE: Bishop Dantiscus would like to be your friend.

COPERNICUS: Impossible. I detest him.

GIESE: He is simply following orders from Rome.

COPERNICUS: More than that. He never lets you forget he was once the emperor's ambassador to Spain. What does that mean in this little outpost in Poland?

GIESE: But it was a rather illustrious career.

COPERNICUS: He's a pompous ass.

GIESE: Sorry I brought it up. It's time for me to be going. The horses are ready.

COPERNICUS: It was so good to see you again.

GIESE: I'll be back before long. Till then, let me know what happens with Rheticus.

GIESE and COPERNICUS exit.

RHETICUS *(addressing audience):* What is a person to do? I have written my most effusive letters to the man, yet he does not respond. I am—to be frank—the fair-haired boy of the Reformation, being a special favorite of Dr. Melanchthon and not unkindly regarded by Martin Luther himself. Not for my meager talents, nor for my charms—if I have such—but for my thirst for knowledge, my love of truth, my zeal to probe the most exciting realm man ever saw: I mean the stars, the heavens, the dark and silent domain that looms over us as a great mystery.

Great professors admire me; students flock to my classes. Yet this old man at the extreme outskirts of the earth will not even acknowledge me. For nearly forty years, he has worked alone in his tower, keeping secret every discovery he has made. I have written to him three times, but he will not answer me. Therefore I have no choice but to go to Poland and find him.

Scene Two

MELANCHTHON'S *study in Wittenberg.*

MELANCHTHON: No, you may not go to Poland. I won't hear of it.

RHETICUS: If I am to teach astronomy, I must pursue the true nature of the heavens.

MELANCHTHON: Has he invited you to study with him?

RHETICUS: No.

MELANCHTHON: Has he ever invited anyone to study with him?

RHETICUS: Not that I know of.

MELANCHTHON: Remember also that Poland is a Catholic country. As a Lutheran you will not be welcomed there. Indeed, it could dangerous for you. *(RHETICUS attempts to speak, but Melanchthon stops him.)* And furthermore, I just granted you leave to study with Peter Apian and Philip Imser. You were gone for three months. Now you want to take off again.

RHETICUS: He has a new theory.

MELANCHTHON: He had a new theory when I was your age.

RHETICUS: You knew about him?

MELANCHTHON: Yes. He had circulated a letter to certain astronomers, but he would never publish his findings.

RHETICUS: I wonder why.

MELANCHTHON: Who can say? It doesn't matter anyway. The earth does not move.

RHETICUS: It's worth investigating.

MELANCHTHON: The earth does not move.

RHETICUS: I want to study with Dr. Copernicus.

MELANCHTHON: I don't know what it is you're looking for. You chase about Europe, throwing yourself at every scientist who dreams up a new theory. It's almost unseemly.

RHETICUS: I'm serious, sir.

MELANCHTHON: Think of us here at Wittenberg. We've missed you. You stayed away for months and don't seem to care how we feel.

RHETICUS: What if Copernicus is right? He might completely change the way we see the world.

MELANCHTHON points to planetary chart on wall.

MELANCHTHON: The earth is the center of creation, surrounded by the planets, the stars, and God in his heaven. This is what people believe and what they will continue to believe.

RHETICUS: This scheme that you believe in was not designed by God. It was designed by Ptolemy, in the second century. Every astronomer knows that it's a fiction. He simply devised a scheme which matches what our eyes can see. His model is about appearances, not reality.

MELANCHTHON: Ptolemy described the universe as God created it. We have no choice but to accept it.

RHETICUS: I recall that you taught us to be fearless in our quest for the truth.

MELANCHTHON: In your quest for scientific truth. We encourage astronomers to formulate theoretical models of the universe; it exercises the intellect; it produces better calendars. But it is immoral to suggest that scientific theories actually apply to everyday life. This is the problem with Copernicus. People see the sun rise; they see the sun set. And he would tell them that their eyes deceive them!

RHETICUS: I am sure he seeks to portray the universe as God created it.

MELANCHTHON: Which do you think is more important: to reveal the mysteries of the heavens or to build a world where we can all live in peace and faith and contentment?

RHETICUS: They're both important. Surely one does not rule out the other.

MELANCHTHON: There is little in heaven or on earth as simple as we would wish. Look at this Reformation of ours. It was meant to simplify Christianity. We believed the Roman church had become a prison, with God as its prisoner. We wanted to free him. So we translated Holy Scripture into German and taught men and women to read. Now they may communicate directly with God through faith in our Savior. They no longer depend on priests; they needn't buy indulgences for their sins. But I wonder now if we were wrong. Instead of a prison, the church may have been more of a protective wall...

RHETICUS: Against God?

MELANCHTHON: Against all that we can't know.

RHETICUS (brightly): That is the goal of our work. To find out what we don't know. I never fail to remind my students of the words of Socrates: "The only good is knowledge; the only evil is ignorance."

MELANCHTHON: You are so young.

RHETICUS: And you seem so sad.

MELANCHTHON: I am sad that you want to leave. Sad that what had seemed so hopeful and beautiful has become so ugly and painful. And we have broken the Lord's church in half.

RHETICUS: Perhaps we can still reconcile with Rome.

MELANCHTHON: Let us hope for it. Sometimes I think Luther has made a terrible mistake, and then all my doubts set in.

I cannot sleep, and try in vain to pray, longing to be restored to good and simple faith. This is something I've not spoken of before. And certainly not to Luther.

RHETICUS: I think my teacher's planet has passed into an unsympathetic house.

MELANCHTHON: Spare me your astrology. I'm so glad you're back. We've all missed you.

RHETICUS: As I missed you. Which makes it harder to ask your permission to go to Poland.

MELANCHTHON: You have responsibilities here. Your classes begin next month.

RHETICUS: My colleagues have agreed to take my classes. I promise to return for the spring term.

MELANCHTHON: I don't understand you. You're head of the mathematics department. You are respected and loved by many people. You could spend the rest of your life here in contentment.

RHETICUS: I would go mad from contentment. I am a scientist and a seeker.

MELANCHTHON: Yet you keep edging toward heresy.

RHETICUS: I am edging toward the truth. I would like to go with your permission and your blessing.

MELANCHTHON: You agree to return for the spring class?

RHETICUS: I do.

MELANCHTHON: Very well, you may go.

RHETICUS: Thank you, sir. You won't regret this.

Scene Three

COPERNICUS *sits at his desk in his study in Frauenberg.* ANNA *enters.*

ANNA: You got another letter from the Lutheran in Wittenberg. (COPERNICUS *doesn't take letter; she drops it on table.*) You could at least answer him.

COPERNICUS: Anna, there's something I must say to you.

A pause, as ANNA *waits for him to speak.*

ANNA: Very well. What is it?

COPERNICUS: Bishop Dantiscus. He has issued an order. All women are to leave this cathedral chapter.

ANNA: Leave? Why?

COPERNICUS: The bishop wants it.

ANNA: When?

COPERNICUS: Immediately.

ANNA: It's impossible. This is too sudden.

COPERNICUS: It's not sudden. He wanted you to leave a year ago.

ANNA: Why didn't you tell me?

COPERNICUS: I hoped he might relent.

ANNA: But the other canons have women. Some have children. What will become of us? Where will we go?

COPERNICUS: He is quite firm. The church must live by its rules.

ANNA: But you're not a priest.

COPERNICUS: The rules apply to canons as well. We must set an example.

ANNA: Example! The bishop makes no secret of his own bastard children. Why must he persecute innocent women?

COPERNICUS: The bishop has spoken.

ANNA: What wrong have I done?

COPERNICUS: Nothing. I tried to make him understand. I argued for your sake.

ANNA: Then argue some more.

COPERNICUS: I'm too old for these battles.

ANNA: You're not too old.

COPERNICUS: I do not defy my superiors. You must leave.

ANNA: He may be your superior, but he has no power over me. I will not leave. *(She pauses for response; there is none.)* Do you think Canon Sculteti will fold his hands so meekly and say, "Yes, Bishop, of course, Bishop, I'll gladly throw my woman out on the streets?"

COPERNICUS: Sculteti will get into trouble.

ANNA: Is that all you can say? Is that my reward for eight years of companionship? I have given up hope that I might have a husband and children and a life among ordinary people. And you tell me you don't want to get into trouble.

COPERNICUS: I am not ungrateful. I have never been ungrateful. Try to understand. You must go back to Danzig, back to your family.

ANNA: I won't be thrown out like a pair of old shoes.

COPERNICUS: We must live according to rules even when they make us unhappy.

ANNA: Why are you doing this?

COPERNICUS: I did all I could. Forgive me for not telling you sooner. It is best that you go back to your family.

ANNA: My family doesn't want me.

COPERNICUS: You have an income. I'll support you as long as I live. Go somewhere else, to another town. You could even marry.

ANNA: I am married, in my heart. *(She stares at* COPERNICUS.*)* I have been a fool.

COPERNICUS: I tried, Anna. I did all that I could.

ANNA: Who do you think would marry me?

COPERNICUS: A widower, perhaps. In another town. A man younger than myself.

ANNA: I can't see it.

COPERNICUS: Even if the bishop had not intervened, you must have a plan for yourself. I am an old man. I am not well. I will die before very few years have passed.

ANNA: I have a plan. When the time comes, when there is nothing else left for me, I will go back to my family.

COPERNICUS: Good.

Scene Four

COPERNICUS'S study. RHETICUS, dressed now in colorful, almost gaudy clothes, with a feather in his cap, knocks on the door, which KARL opens.

RHETICUS: Karl! What are you doing here?

KARL: I do some work for the doctor.

RHETICUS: You're not working at the inn?

KARL: I'm still there. He needs help now that he sent his woman away. Don't look so alarmed. He doesn't know anything about you and me.

RHETICUS: That's nobody's business but our own. I came here to see Dr. Copernicus.

KARL: That's not possible.

RHETICUS: He's out? Then I'll wait for him.

KARL: He's not out. He doesn't want visitors.

RHETICUS *(grandly)*: I am Professor Georg Joachim Rheticus from the University of Wittenberg. I have written Dr. Copernicus to inform him of my arrival.

KARL: Yes, he got your letter. He doesn't want to see you.

RHETICUS: Why not?

KARL: My guess would be that he doesn't want to make the bishop angry.

RHETICUS: What does that have to do with me?

KARL: You're a Lutheran, right? This is a Catholic country. The bishop said Lutherans will be burned at the stake. What do you think of that?

RHETICUS: Who is this bishop?

KARL: Bishop Dantiscus.

RHETICUS: Where can I find him?

KARL: Just across the courtyard.

RHETICUS: Thank you. I'll find my way out.

> *RHETICUS crosses stage, where lights reveal DANTISCUS, rising from his desk..*

DANTISCUS: Well, my young man, you are certainly a fish out of water. It's not every day we see the arrival of a professor from the very center of heresy.

RHETICUS: Your Excellency, I humbly welcome your greetings. It is not my intention to offend the beliefs of anyone, especially one so august and renowned as yourself. However, it seems that Lutherans are not allowed in this land. Surely this is not true.

DANTISCUS: They're not at all welcome. Now tell me what you're doing here.

RHETICUS: I came here to meet Dr. Copernicus.

DANTISCUS: Copernicus. I'm surprised he invited you.

RHETICUS: He didn't.

DANTISCUS: You came all the way from Wittenberg, uninvited, unannounced—that's quite remarkable.

RHETICUS: Perhaps I am reckless, but it seemed the only way. I have to meet him.

DANTISCUS: Why do you have to meet him?

RHETICUS: He has a new theory of the heavens.

DANTISCUS: Yes, he has a theory, and he won't tell anyone about it. We have beseeched him. Even Cardinal Schoenberg—the pope's private secretary—has all but begged him to share his discoveries. The Church, you know, is quite supportive of the new astronomy. The calendar is a shambles. Last year Easter fell two weeks after Christmas. It was most difficult to observe Lent while celebrating Our Lord's birth. We hope Copernicus might be able to correct such errors. But he refuses all requests. He is a very difficult man. Now let me offer a word of caution: you are visiting hostile territory.

RHETICUS: I'm beginning to see that.

DANTISCUS: You are a Lutheran in a Catholic country. Just this morning I signed another edict condemning Lutherans. If I were to be rigorous, I should have you banished at once.

RHETICUS: Your Excellency!

DANTISCUS searches through some papers.

DANTISCUS: Here. *(He looks more closely.)* No, this one is against parting the hair.

RHETICUS: Parting the hair?

DANTISCUS: A revolting new fashion that has crept in from Italy. The people have an insatiable appetite for novelty. Here it is. "All believers in the Lutheran heresy are to be banished from this land at once. Heretics remaining in this town will be burned at the stake." You needn't turn pale, my boy. These edicts apply only to the common people. I would no more dream of burning a mathematician than you would. I wouldn't even object if you parted your hair.

RHETICUS: Maybe I will.

DANTISCUS: Let me offer some friendly advice. It was brought to my attention that the bailiff nearly hauled you off last night.

RHETICUS: "I entered the grotto where vice beckoned."

DANTISCUS (startled): I beg your pardon?

RHETICUS (quoting): "I entered the grotto where vice beckoned In drunken frenzy I possessed them all I missed none…"

DANTISCUS *(pleased):* I was quite young when I wrote that.

RHETICUS: Your poems are very popular among the undergraduates.

DANTISCUS: These days I write only sacred verse. What actually happened last night?

RHETICUS: Nothing, really. I was at the inn and encountered some boisterous fellows who inflamed me with their absurd notions.

DANTISCUS: Such as?

RHETICUS: They claimed that Dr. Copernicus is a sorcerer. Can you imagine that? They are completely ignorant. Naturally, I had to oppose them.

DANTISCUS: Had you been drinking?

RHETICUS: "I entered the grotto where vice beckoned."

DANTISCUS: Well, don't enter it too often. It will be a pleasure to have you among us, so I would not want an untoward incident to disrupt your visit.

RHETICUS: I will be the soul of discretion.

DANTISCUS *(skeptical):* Try, at any rate. I should tell you that Dr. Melanchthon has sent me a letter regarding your visit. He seems to think very highly of your abilities.

RHETICUS: Did he really?

DANTISCUS: You seem surprised.

RHETICUS: Dr. Melanchthon has been like a father to me. But he discouraged me from making this trip. He doesn't want to change the world.

DANTISCUS: And you think Copernicus does?

RHETICUS: I think he must.

DANTISCUS: When you meet Dr. Copernicus, you will discover that he wants to change nothing.

RHETICUS: He has refused to meet me.

DANTISCUS: Really?

RHETICUS: If Your Excellency could arrange an introduction, I would be most grateful.

DANTISCUS: I'll speak to him. Now, we can't have you staying at the inn. Bring your things to the chapter house; I'll have a room made ready for you.

RHETICUS: Your Excellency is too generous!

DANTISCUS (waving off praise): The pleasure is mine. Now, would you care to see my new astrolabe?

RHETICUS: You observe the stars?

DANTISCUS: As an amateur only.

RHETICUS: Splendid. And about the introduction to Dr. Copernicus?

DANTISCUS: He will be delighted to greet you. I will make sure of it.

Scene Five

KARL and COPERNICUS in Copernicus's study.

KARL: He's here.

COPERNICUS: I may as well get this over with. What's he like?

KARL: He talks a lot.

COPERNICUS: One of those. Send him in.

KARL exits. RHETICUS enters, again in colorful costume, carrying a leather bag. He gazes in awe at Copernicus and drops to one knee. COPERNICUS is taken aback at this display.

RHETICUS: Doctor Copernicus! *Domine Praeceptor!*

COPERNICUS: Please stand up.

RHETICUS: So may the gods love me, I have never been greeted with kinder or more pleasing words. Dr. Copernicus, I am Georg Joachim Rheticus, lately of Wittenberg, professor of mathematics and student of the stars.

COPERNICUS: I know who you are. Now please get up.

RHETICUS stands up.

RHETICUS: Your fame is of such exceeding—

COPERNICUS *(alarmed)*: My fame!

RHETICUS: Your *esteem* among a very small, very select group of astronomers has brought me here to seek you.

COPERNICUS: I am honored, but I must tell you now that I have never taken on students.

RHETICUS: I have come all the way from Wittenberg.

COPERNICUS: It was reckless of you. Our bishop does not permit Lutherans in this district.

RHETICUS: I have met Bishop Dantiscus. He is a most gracious man.

COPERNICUS: You think so?

RHETICUS: He has shown me great courtesy. Everywhere I go, I find a warm welcome. This is a most hospitable land.

COPERNICUS: How lovely.

RHETICUS: Did you receive the treatise I sent you?

COPERNICUS: Yes. You seem to have a thorough grasp of geometry.

RHETICUS: Thank you. I have felt, since I was a boy, an abiding love for angles.

An awkward pause, and for once RHETICUS *doesn't have anything to say.*

COPERNICUS: Well, my young professor, I have several duties to attend to. I appreciate the honor you do me by traveling such a long distance, and I wish you a safe return.

RHETICUS: A safe return? I just got here.

COPERNICUS: I don't see that we have any more business to attend to.

RHETICUS: You mean I have to go?

COPERNICUS: To be blunt, yes, you have to go.

RHETICUS: But your theory! I came here for your theory.

COPERNICUS: I know that. But you were not invited here, and as a Lutheran cannot be welcomed.

RHETICUS: Can I meet you again tomorrow?

COPERNICUS: No.

RHETICUS: Day after tomorrow?

COPERNICUS: Professor Rheticus, you should return to Wittenberg.

RHETICUS: Perhaps I didn't make myself clear. I have traveled a great distance, avoided highwaymen, slept in haylofts—because I believe you are a man who has much to offer the world. I came here to learn from you.

COPERNICUS: You came here to appropriate my life's work, to seize it as your own, to amuse yourself. I have not been waiting for a student. I admire your spirit, but I do not accept your offer. You have come to the wrong person.

RHETICUS *(temporizing):* Well, we needn't get into your theory. Perhaps we could discuss the new maps being drawn. Don't you find Waldseemüller's work intriguing?

COPERNICUS: I am not interested in the new world.

RHETICUS: And why should you be, when there are such astounding discoveries here in the old world? My students cannot cease to marvel over—

COPERNICUS *(interrupting):* Dr. Rheticus, forgive me if I am being rude, but there is no reason to continue this visit. You may go now.

RHETICUS: I see.

RHETICUS, *downcast and disappointed, turns to exit.*

COPERNICUS: You forgot your bag.

RHETICUS *brightens, remembering his intention.*

RHETICUS: And so I did. *(He removes books from his bag.)* I brought these for you. Euclid, in the original Greek.

COPERNICUS *(moved and impressed):* Euclid. I didn't know it had been published.

RHETICUS: Just a month ago. And here is Ptolemy, in Greek. First edition! And some lesser works by our living mathematicians.

COPERNICUS: These are wonderful gifts. *(He regards Rheticus thoughtfully.)* How did you hear about me?

RHETICUS: From Peter Apian.

COPERNICUS: What is Apian up to these days?

RHETICUS: He is drawing up maps of America.

COPERNICUS: Really? And what are the other mathematicians doing?

RHETICUS: Everything. Pursuing the study of triangles, building new observatories, devising the new calendar. ...moving the sun to the center of the universe.

COPERNICUS: I had assumed that everyone was at work on the church calendar.

RHETICUS: Many are. It seems to be holding up still.

COPERNICUS: It won't hold up for long. And I suspect you know why.

RHETICUS: Yes. Because we are still beholden to Ptolemy—and this closed, constricted universe he gave us. You are the man who will open it up.

COPERNICUS: Why do you say that?

RHETICUS: An astronomer with your depth of knowledge would see that Ptolemy was wrong, and as a seeker of Truth, you would rejoice in finding the true design of the universe.

COPERNICUS: Nonsense! I didn't think Ptolemy was wrong. I just wanted to clean up his errors. There were too many loose ends, too many sloppy calculations.

RHETICUS: Then something must have happened.

COPERNICUS: Dr. Rheticus, how are planets supposed to move?

RHETICUS: In perfect spheres at uniform speed.

COPERNICUS: Exactly. So we have a problem. When you observe Mars, it seems to move back and forth in the sky, to start and stop. Hardly a perfect sphere at a uniform speed.

RHETICUS: Those movements are accounted for by the epicycles.

COPERNICUS: Yes, epicycles are quite ingenious. Ptolemy managed to save the appearances—but do you believe epicycles exist in reality?

RHETICUS: Of course not. No astronomer does. But they do save the appearances.

COPERNICUS: Then we have a problem. Look at Mars. With all those epicycles, it must fly about like a pinwheel. I wanted a more orderly solution, without those untidy epicycles.

RHETICUS: Then how do you account for its movement?

COPERNICUS: Suppose the sun were the center of the universe. If you were to observe all the planets, including Earth, from the sun, there would be no retrogressions.

RHETICUS: Because...?

COPERNICUS: Put the sun at the center. Then Mercury, Venus, Earth, Mars—

RHETICUS (comprehending): Our perceptions will change. With a smaller orbit than Mars, the Earth will approach it and then overtake it.

COPERNICUS: Which causes it to appear that Mars is moving backward.

RHETICUS: It's so simple! Why has no one thought of this before?

COPERNICUS: They have. But no one wants to believe that the earth itself moves. It defies the evidence of our senses. We see the sun rise and set. We feel no movement under our feet. The very idea is absurd.

RHETICUS: But it's true.

COPERNICUS: It is.

RHETICUS: Why have you kept your theory a secret?

COPERNICUS: Because I can't prove it.

RHETICUS: But it is correct?

COPERNICUS: I know it's correct. I just haven't been able to get all the pieces to fit together.

RHETICUS: Then we will work out the proofs.

COPERNICUS: We?

RHETICUS: If Your Most Learned Excellency will permit me to assist you.

COPERNICUS: It is a huge undertaking.

RHETICUS: I'm ready.

COPERNICUS: I have many other duties—the sick must be tended, the chapter's affairs demand my time, I promised to make a map of Prussia for Duke Albrecht; it's two years overdue.

RHETICUS: Let me do it. I love to make maps!

COPERNICUS: The land has to be surveyed first.

RHETICUS: I love to survey land!

COPERNICUS: Are you always so eager?

RHETICUS: Always.

COPERNICUS: I would never have imagined you as a student of the stars.

RHETICUS: What would you imagine?

COPERNICUS: A man with a more solemn mind, who chose more sober dress, who was not so quick to embrace a new theory.

RHETICUS: I will be the best student you could ever hope for.

COPERNICUS *regards* RHETICUS *thoughtfully.*

COPERNICUS: Very well. You'll be needing a place to stay.

RHETICUS: Bishop Dantiscus has kindly lodged me by the cathedral.

COPERNICUS: Oh, he has?

RHETICUS: He has a new astrolabe there.

COPERNICUS: The bishop and his toys. You'll be much better suited in my quarters. Will you stay here as my guest?

RHETICUS: Certainly.

COPERNICUS: Good. Karl! *(KARL enters.)* Karl, Dr. Rheticus will be staying here as my guest. Please bring his things from the inn and put them in the spare room.

KARL: Fraulein Anna's room?

COPERNICUS: Yes. *(KARL exits.* COPERNICUS *gives a small manuscript to* RHETICUS.*)* And you may read this.

RHETICUS: Is this your theory?

COPERNICUS: No. It is a paper I circulated some years ago. It will give you a general idea of the theory.

RHETICUS: When may I see your manuscript?

COPERNICUS: We'll see. Read this first.

RHETICUS: I'll read it today.

Scene Six

RHETICUS in his room with manuscript. KARL enters.

RHETICUS: Tell me, Karl. How long have you worked for Dr. Copernicus?

KARL: A couple of weeks. Ever since the fraulein had to leave.

RHETICUS: Will you keep working at the tavern?

KARL: Yes, but I don't like it there. I'm thinking of looking for a real job. Maybe in Gdansk.

RHETICUS: What will you do?

KARL: I could work at the harbor. Or with a weaver. I'll find something.

RHETICUS *(putting away manuscript)*: I wish you were a mathematician so I could tell you about this.

KARL: He says the earth moves around the sun, doesn't he?

RHETICUS: Actually, the earth revolves around the eccentric, a point in space near the sun. But that's just a technicality. For practical purposes we can say the earth moves around the sun.

KARL: That's what I thought he said.

RHETICUS: But if the earth moves, there is no longer a need for epicycles. Do you know what epicycles are?

KARL: No.

RHETICUS: Then you shall have a lesson in sky geometry. Observe: I want the apple on the table. I walk across the room and pick it up. *(He does so.)* That is a simple movement, clean and elegant, which is how a planet should move. But when we observe Mars, this is what we see. *(He demonstrates the erratic appearance of Mars's orbit, starting forward, stopping, backing up, going forward again, to pick up apple.)*

KARL: Weird.

RHETICUS: Exactly. So our ancient astronomers had an idea. Suppose that in order to get to the apple, I have to do this. *(RHETICUS adds a loop to his walk across the room.)* That would be an epicycle.

KARL: But why do it?

RHETICUS: In order to solve a problem. Obviously, God would not create a a silly universe, with planets jumping wildly all over the place. So our wise astronomers devised a series of loops and flourishes to give reason to such erratic movement. Imagine that I am Mars. You be the earth. Sit right there, pleased with yourself... *(KARL sits on bench)* while I, Mars, who make no claim to be the center of the universe, begin my orbit. *(RHETICUS moves in a large arc upstage.)* I go forward; you see me on your left side. Now I move backward. *(He moves backward.)*

KARL: You're on my right side.

RHETICUS: Obviously something is wrong with this planet.

KARL: I guess.

RHETICUS: Now let me add epicycles. I continue to move forward, but Ptolemy tells me I must add this contraption to my orbit. *(RHETICUS begins to add a loop to his arc.)* Now where do you see me?

KARL: On my left.

RHETICUS continues his loop.

RHETICUS: Now where am I?

KARL: On my right.

RHETICUS: Just as if I had gone forward and then backward.

KARL: So that explains it.

RHETICUS: It explains nothing. Epicycles do not exist.

35

KARL: Oh.

RHETICUS: But now let us say this chair is the center of the universe. Let us call it the sun. You, little Earth, will perform your orbit, and Mars will perform his orbit, both of them perfect circles. Begin. *(KARL, three feet away from chair, and RHETICUS, eight feet away, begin to walk in a circle around the chair.)* What is happening?

KARL: I'm moving around the chair faster than you are.

RHETICUS: Because your orbit is smaller. What else happens?

KARL: I don't see anything else.

RHETICUS: Look at Mars, at me. Now I am on your left. *(They continue to circle.)*

KARL: And now you're on my right.

RHETICUS *(stops moving)*: Am I moving backward and forward?

KARL: No.

RHETICUS: Am I turning cartwheels in space?

KARL: No.

RHETICUS: Am I about to discover the true nature of the universe?

KARL: What?

RHETICUS: Karl, the world has never seen anything like this before. And I am here when it all begins to happen.

KARL: And what if the planets were to move like this? *(KARL glides up to* RHETICUS, *makes loop around him, and embraces him.)*

RHETICUS (pushing him away): That would be against the laws of nature.

KARL: Oh, really?

RHETICUS: Yes. You traversed from there to here in the form of an ellipse. Planets don't move in ellipses. They move in circles.

KARL: What makes you so sure?

RHETICUS: Aristotle.

KARL: Forget the planets. Let's talk about you and me. You seemed to enjoy my company last week.

RHETICUS: Last week I was staying at the inn. Now I'm a guest of Dr. Copernicus.

KARL: He won't know.

RHETICUS: I came here to study, not to play.

KARL: I thought you liked me.

RHETICUS: I like you very much, but I am interested only in Dr. Copernicus.

KARL: You're making a mistake there. He only likes women.

RHETICUS: I mean his work. I am interested in his work. *(KARL, not put off, tries to embrace RHETICUS, who steps aside.)* Even if I wanted you to stay—

KARL: Which you do.

RHETICUS: It's impossible. I'm working with the doctor tonight.

KARL: You know you want to.

RHETICUS: Maybe it would be a good idea if you did leave Frauenberg.

KARL: Now you want to get rid of me?

RHETICUS: Yes! I've got work to do. Now, be a good boy, and go on your way.

KARL: I'll be back later.

RHETICUS: I'm sure you will.

KARL exits.

Scene Seven

RHETICUS and COPERNICUS on wooden platform outside his study. The platform runs along the rampart that defends the cathedral compound. They are recording observations of the planets. Their only tool is a triquetum, a simple device made of three slats of wood. It is near dawn.

COPERNICUS: Deferent?

RHETICUS: Thirty degrees.

COPERNICUS: Eccentric?

RHETICUS: Six degrees.

COPERNICUS: Excellent.

RHETICUS: Mercury fits in, just as you predicted it would.

COPERNICUS: I wish Ptolemy could see this. I haven't enjoyed myself this much since the solar eclipse of 1520.

RHETICUS: Now what?

COPERNICUS: We wait for Mars. If he aligns with Mercury, then we will have the proof we need. Where is Mars now?

RHETICUS: Twenty-eight degrees.

COPERNICUS: It will take only a few more minutes.

RHETICUS: Who was your favorite teacher?

COPERNICUS: I don't think I had a favorite.

RHETICUS: Which one did you admire most?

COPERNICUS: I admired them all.

RHETICUS, stymied, plunges ahead.

RHETICUS: Isn't this a wonderful age we're living in?

COPERNICUS: Wonderful? In what way?

RHETICUS: Well, for one, the new world.

COPERNICUS: America.

RHETICUS: Doesn't that excite you?

COPERNICUS: No.

RHETICUS: I think it's extremely exciting. And we have an explosion of books now.

COPERNICUS: Yes, the printing press is quite remarkable. Books are wonderful. The problem is that anyone can get them. Ignorant people have started reading. They start to think.

RHETICUS: But isn't that a good thing?

COPERNICUS: It's terrible. The vast majority of people are incapable of understanding the simplest ideas. They should never be allowed to read books.

RHETICUS (a bit shocked): Dr. Copernicus, you leave me speechless.

COPERNICUS: I find that hard to believe. Where is Mars now?

RHETICUS studies position of triquetum.

RHETICUS: Twenty-nine degrees.

COPERNICUS: As it should be.

RHETICUS: Do you make observations very often?

COPERNICUS: No. But since you're here, I thought it might be rather entertaining for you.

A pause.

RHETICUS: Have you ever seen a man beheaded?

COPERNICUS: That's an unusual question.

RHETICUS: My father was beheaded. I was fourteen when it happened.

COPERNICUS: What was his crime?

RHETICUS: Nothing. People accused him of sorcery, but it wasn't true. He was a physician, like yourself.

COPERNICUS is silent for a moment.

COPERNICUS: Both my parents died before I was ten.

RHETICUS: Where did you go?

COPERNICUS: My uncle, who was bishop of this very cathedral, took me and Andreas under his wing.

RHETICUS: Who was Andreas?

COPERNICUS: My brother, two years older. The bishop provided us with the best possible education and then arranged for us to become canons of the cathedral—a lifetime income, so long as we stayed here.

RHETICUS: Is your brother here?

COPERNICUS: He died in Rome years ago.

RHETICUS: So he gave up his income. That was bold of him.

COPERNICUS: Not exactly. We paid him to stay away. Where is Mars now?

RHETICUS: Twenty-nine degrees, fifteen minutes. Why did you pay Andreas to stay away?

COPERNICUS: He whored and drank and flaunted his licentious ways. It ended with the pox. His face was disfigured, monstrous, yet he went about as if he were blameless. He had no shame.

RHETICUS: That's when he went to Rome?

COPERNICUS: Only after the chapter voted to disown him. We tried to cut off his income, too, but the pope wouldn't let us.

RHETICUS: You voted to disown your brother?

COPERNICUS: Gladly. He did just as he pleased. I haven't thought about my brother for years. Now where is Mars?

RHETICUS: Twenty-eight degrees.

COPERNICUS (*frustrated*): What is wrong with that planet? Going backwards again.

RHETICUS: I'm sure we can find the solution.

COPERNICUS: How?

RHETICUS: Perhaps if you will let me study your manuscript—

COPERNICUS: No. You're not ready for it. I'm not ready.

RHETICUS: I'm sure I will understand it.

COPERNICUS: The mathematics, yes. You'll understand the mathematics. But there is much more unwritten and unsaid.

RHETICUS: I think you should have it published in Nuremberg. I know it's a Lutheran city, but the best printing presses are there.

COPERNICUS *(incredulous)*: What makes you think I am going to publish?

RHETICUS: Surely you will. I assumed—

COPERNICUS: You assumed incorrectly. I have no intention of publishing my theory.

RHETICUS: But you must! You must share it with other scientists.

COPERNICUS: I have thought over the matter for many years now. I see no reason to publish.

RHETICUS: But that's preposterous—not publishing!

COPERNICUS: It is not preposterous. Have you not learned that knowledge is sacred? To publish my theory would be comparable to pouring pure, clean water into a dirty well: the pure water would be wasted, and the dirt would only get agitated.

RHETICUS: Do you regard other scientists as dirt at the bottom of a well?

COPERNICUS: Sometimes I do.

RHETICUS: But your theory will change the way we see everything.

COPERNICUS: I don't want to change anything. I have no zeal for declaring the old world dead. I have always lived in that world. I shall miss it.

RHETICUS: You should rejoice that God chose you to be the father of a new age.

COPERNICUS (almost amused): God chose me?

RHETICUS: Yes, you.

COPERNICUS: And you would force me to carry this burden?

RHETICUS: I will help you.

COPERNICUS: Perhaps. We shall see.

Scene Eight

DANTISCUS enters Copernicus's study.

DANTISCUS: I have to talk to you.

COPERNICUS: Yes, Your Lordship. I trust I have not offended you. The woman is gone; she no longer lives here.

DANTISCUS: It's not about Anna. It's Rheticus.

COPERNICUS: Rheticus? I thought you approved his visit.

DANTISCUS: I did. I was happy to welcome a scientist and professor. But he was almost arrested yesterday.

COPERNICUS: For what?

DANTISCUS: Sodomy. The night watchman discovered him and Karl behind the inn. I was able to intervene, so no action will be taken against him.

COPERNICUS: And he's a Lutheran as well.

DANTISCUS: Yes, he's guilty of two capital offenses.

COPERNICUS: There could be a scandal.

DANTISCUS: If word gets out. My advice would be to send him away.

COPERNICUS: With all respect, I humbly beseech you not to send him away. He has a good mind; he understands my work.

DANTISCUS: True, he's bright. But he seems to have a fondness for undesirable people. It's been noticed. It's bound to happen again.

COPERNICUS: I understand. I could take him to visit my friend Bishop Giese. That might be a good plan.

DANTISCUS: Bishop Giese would want him?

COPERNICUS: Just for a visit. A few weeks.

DANTISCUS: That would give us time for things to cool off here. Yes, take him away for a few weeks.

COPERNICUS: It's unfortunate.

DANTISCUS: Yes, he has so much promise.

> *DANTISCUS exits. COPERNICUS goes to his desk, tries to work, becomes restless, and begins to pace. RHETICUS enters.*

RHETICUS: Shall we observe the stars tonight?

COPERNICUS: I think not. Perhaps we should have made observations last night.

RHETICUS: It was cloudy last night.

COPERNICUS: The bishop has told me where you were last night. There could be a dreadful scandal.

RHETICUS: It was nothing.

COPERNICUS: Nothing? You were nearly arrested.

RHETICUS (blithely): Well, yes, it got a bit sticky for a moment there, but all is well now.

COPERNICUS: All is not well.

RHETICUS: I'm sorry if I have offended you.

COPERNICUS: You have offended the noble and sacred domain of Science. I had almost come to believe that you were a serious student.

RHETICUS: I am serious.

COPERNICUS: But you indulge yourself. You spend your evenings with rude and ignorant fellows. You flout the rules of decent behavior.

RHETICUS: You know that I have dedicated my heart and soul to our search for astronomical truth.

COPERNICUS: Then accept the gravity of your mission. When you seek to uncover eternal truth—truth that we conceive only with the greatest daring and utter with the greatest fear—your behavior must be exalted. You must exceed other men in stamina, in courage, and in faith. I had expected so much from you. Not wanton dissipation.

RHETICUS: I sincerely apologize if I have offended the honor of Science.

COPERNICUS: I had hoped I could trust you with my theory.

RHETICUS: You know that you can trust me.

COPERNICUS: For what purpose? For you to debauch yourself with servants? What will people say?

RHETICUS: They'll say you're not a sorcerer.

COPERNICUS: What?

RHETICUS: The villagers—they think you're a sorcerer. They think you cast spells and concoct magic potions.

COPERNICUS: Nonsense.

RHETICUS: I know it's nonsense. But they don't. And I don't want it to happen again.

COPERNICUS: Don't confuse me with your father.

RHETICUS: You needn't worry about that. My father had the courage of his convictions.

COPERNICUS: Perhaps he did. But if he had been more cautious he might be alive today.

RHETICUS glares at COPERNICUS then exits.

Scene Nine

Later that night. RHETICUS *sits on his bed, playing a mandolin, in candlelight.* KARL *enters.*

KARL: Do you need anything?

RHETICUS: No.

KARL: The doctor was really angry at you.

RHETICUS: I'm thinking of going back to Wittenberg.

KARL: I wish you wouldn't.

RHETICUS: He wouldn't care. He'd be relieved. He could carry his book to his grave, without me pestering him to publish. He doesn't want me here.

KARL: I think he does.

RHETICUS: He won't show me his book. He thinks I'm dissolute. And what of it? More than anybody else, I understand his work.

KARL sits beside RHETICUS *and takes his hand.*

KARL: He'll come round. In a day or two you'll forget this ever happened.

RHETICUS: In a day or two I might not be here.

KARL: You'll feel better tomorrow.

RHETICUS: Easy for you to say.

KARL: Come on. It can't be that bad.

RHETICUS: I have done everything I can to win this old man over. He's like an iceberg.

KARL: He's a tough old bird, for sure. Get some sleep. You'll feel better.

KARL rises to leave, but RHETICUS keeps his hand.

RHETICUS: Don't go.

KARL looks at RHETICUS for a moment, hesitating, then puts out candle and gets into bed.

Lights reveal COPERNICUS pacing his study. He takes out manuscript and worries over it. Carrying manuscript, he walks out on dimly lit rampart. DANTISCUS enters.

DANTISCUS: Good evening, Dr. Copernicus.

COPERNICUS: Your Lordship. I've never seen you here before.

DANTISCUS: I walk here sometimes when I feel overcome with questions. Small questions, not great ones. Why are we here in Poland instead of in Italy? Why am I a bishop instead of a cobbler? Why do we live at all? Oedipus said it is better not to have been born. Do you agree?

COPERNICUS: Yes. It is much better not to be born.

DANTISCUS: What did you tell Rheticus?

COPERNICUS: Not much.

DANTISCUS: Will you take him to visit your friend?

COPERNICUS: Yes. I suppose.

DANTISCUS: What are you waiting for?

COPERNICUS: I'm tired.

DANTISCUS: You need to get him out of here for a while.

COPERNICUS: As Your Excellency wishes.

DANTISCUS: Why do you hate me?

COPERNICUS: Why do you torment me?

DANTISCUS: I don't torment you. I am the bishop of this cathedral. It is my duty to carry out the church's rules. I am sorry about your woman. I'm sorry she was so important to you. What are you carrying?

COPERNICUS: My new system of the universe.

DANTISCUS: Why did you bring it here?

COPERNICUS: I must decide whether or not to show it to Rheticus.

DANTISCUS: Give it to him. It's what he lives for now.

COPERNICUS: So it appears. You may wonder why life made you a bishop rather than a cobbler. I wonder why my life has brought me to an impossible choice: either I surrender my life's work to a youngster I neither trust nor admire or I drop it in the river.

DANTISCUS: Don't do that. We want to see it. We want to know the truth.

COPERNICUS: No, you don't.

DANTISCUS: But we do. Knowledge is a manifestation of God.

COPERNICUS: That's what I thought, too. Now I'm not so sure.

DANTISCUS: Do you believe your book holds some truth?

COPERNICUS: Yes.

DANTISCUS: Then give it to the world.

COPERNICUS: I am an old man. I can't face the discord it is certain to cause.

DANTISCUS: You have Rheticus. Let him shoulder your burden.

COPERNICUS: He'd like nothing better.

DANTISCUS: I'll speak plainly with you: your theory may have a new truth for us, and it may be more accurate than Ptolemy, but in my heart, I don't believe that we will ever know what this universe is.

COPERNICUS: Then you think it won't make any difference if I publish?

DANTISCUS: Ultimately it won't.

DANTISCUS exits.

COPERNICUS: Ultimately it will.

COPERNICUS goes to RHETICUS'S room and stands in doorway with candle. RHETICUS rises, startled, careful to conceal KARL.

RHETICUS: My teacher...

COPERNICUS: I have brought you the manuscript.

RHETICUS: You trust me—

COPERNICUS: I have reached a dead end. My work will have been in vain unless I can find someone—

RHETICUS: I am here.

COPERNICUS: —someone who understands.

RHETICUS: I am here.

COPERNICUS: I am an old man. You still have much to learn in the ways of stewardship, but there is no one else. You must try, Rheticus.

RHETICUS: I will try.

COPERNICUS: Take it.

COPERNICUS gives manuscript to RHETICUS.

COPERNICUS: I think it is advisable for you to leave this place for a while. I would like to visit my friend Bishop Giese in Löbau. Will you come with me?

RHETICUS: If you wish.

COPERNICUS: We will leave in the morning.

COPERNICUS exits.

RHETICUS *(holding up manuscript)*: De Revolutionibus. The Book of Revolutions. My teacher has given us a new view of the world, accurate and true, eternal and good. He has been God's agent and loyal servant. And God has granted to my learned teacher a boundless kingdom in astronomy. May he rule, guard, and increase it, to the restoration of astronomic truth.

Scene Ten

Löbau Castle. BISHOP GIESE *greets* COPERNICUS *and* RHETICUS. *The room is sparsely furnished.*

GIESE: My good friend, welcome back to Löbau. You had a safe journey?

COPERNICUS: Barely. We were attacked by highwaymen near Marienberg; Rheticus fought them off.

GIESE: What a world we live in. Thieves and vandals wherever we turn. You must be Dr. Rheticus. Nicolas tells me you're quite a gifted astronomer.

RHETICUS: I am but an earnest student of the heavens, Your Excellency.

GIESE: You're too modest.

COPERNICUS: The bishop is a gifted astronomer himself.

GIESE: I'm only an amateur.

RHETICUS: I hope you can help me persuade my teacher to publish his work.

GIESE: I have fought that battle for many years.

COPERNICUS: We've had disagreements, not battles.

GIESE: We'll take that up later. You must want something to eat. Come; you can leave your things in the next room. *(To RHETICUS)* There's no help today. Do you mind taking the bags? And there are provisions in the pantry, if you'll bring those also.

RHETICUS: Gladly.

RHETICUS takes bags and exits.

GIESE: I think it's splendid that Rheticus is working with you.

COPERNICUS: Yes. Imagine: one day he just appeared, this little scientist-puppy, brazen and reckless, the last person I would have taken as a student—and a Lutheran as well. But there he is.

GIESE: You seem to be quite taken with him.

COPERNICUS: He has a good mind, and he works hard. I only wish he were more prudent.

GIESE: He's young.

COPERNICUS: There was nearly a scandal in Frauenberg. He and Karl were found together by the night watchman.

GIESE: Well, it happens.

COPERNICUS: It doesn't matter to me if he likes boys, so long as he keeps it quiet. What I don't like is his determination to announce my theory to the entire world. He doesn't understand that knowledge is sacred.

GIESE: I must say I agree with Rheticus. You should publish.

COPERNICUS: I'm not going to.

GIESE: Nicolas, I've encouraged your work and valued your friendship for thirty years now. I know you're a fearful man, you can be stubborn, but I've never known you to be so miserly. Have you not considered your obligation to future generations of scientists? Is it not true that you have learned from the work of ancient Greek and Arab astronomers?

COPERNICUS: That is true.

GIESE: Then why won't you share your work, as you have shared in theirs?

COPERNICUS: I'll tell you why: They simply described what they saw, the movements of the stars and planets. They used these observations to create calendars and to assist sailors in their navigation. Their work didn't defy appearances; it didn't destroy the universe.

GIESE: And neither will yours. Your fears are much exaggerated. Yes, you may change the design of the heavens, and yes, you may upset believers of the old way. But the human race is capable of absorbing change.

COPERNICUS: I wish I could share your optimism. I wish it were easy to publish this thing.

GIESE: Perhaps Rheticus and I together can persuade you.

COPERNICUS: I don't listen to Rheticus when I want sober advice.

GIESE: Give him a chance. Your theory needs a champion, and he clearly longs to carry your banner. I don't think he will disappoint you.

COPERNICUS: You think not?

GIESE: No. And in the meantime I will pray for his sins.

RHETICUS enters, carrying tray of bread, cheese, and wine.

RHETICUS: May I come in?

GIESE: By all means. You're just the person I want to see. We must gird ourselves for an all-out assault.

RHETICUS: I presume you have been discussing publication.

COPERNICUS takes some food.

GIESE: Our friend will not listen to my entreaties.

COPERNICUS: You put impossible demands on me.

GIESE: I simply ask you not to withhold your knowledge. Your fellow scientists need it. The church needs it.

COPERNICUS: I have told Cardinal Schonberg that I will be glad to assist with the calendar reform.

GIESE: And withhold the theory on which you base the reform?

COPERNICUS: They don't need to know it.

GIESE: Your teacher is afraid, Rheticus. He fears ridicule from the common people. He fears the wrath of bishops and cardinals and the pope. I tell you, Nicolas, these fears are imaginary.

COPERNICUS: They are not imaginary.

RHETICUS: All your friends support you. Even Bishop Dantiscus wants you to publish.

COPERNICUS: Bishop Giese and Dantiscus are enlightened men, not ordinary churchmen. When the Vatican fully realizes what I have done, it will crush me in an instant.

GIESE: Your fears are exaggerated..

COPERNICUS: Have you ever thought out the implications of a sun-centered universe?

GIESE: Yes. A true depiction of the heavens will reveal even further God's greatness.

COPERNICUS: Will it? What will happen if you tell people that the earth is not surrounded by the sun, the planets, the fixed stars, and God in his heaven? What will happen if you tell them the earth has no home, that it floats in an endless orbit never at rest?

RHETICUS: You will have told them the truth. They will rejoice.

COPERNICUS: They won't rejoice. They will feel bereft of order. They will be thrown into confusion. We endure lives of pain and suffering on this earth because we know we will find peace in heaven. But now I must tell them that the earth is already in heaven, orbiting in a sphere just like the other planets. How can we aspire to heaven if we're already there? People need to know where they came from and where they're going. If you destroy this universe we understand, if you send the earth hurtling through space, all authority will be undermined, all institutions will be questioned, all values will be challenged, and we will be plagued with uncertainty and doubt.

RHETICUS: If that is the price we must pay for truth, then let us pay it.

COPERNICUS: Listen to him, Giese. Youth has spoken!

GIESE: Suppose, my friend, that we are indeed ready to accept a new model of the universe.

COPERNICUS: Don't you see what will happen?

RHETICUS: Yes. Man will no longer be the lowest creature in the universe, begging for crumbs in heaven. He will make this earth a paradise; he will endow his fellow man with goodness and learning; he will bring us joy in mathematics and beauty in art; he will take his rightful place on earth as the image of God.

COPERNICUS: And what about God? What becomes of the ninth sphere, the last circle, where God made his home?

RHETICUS: It doesn't exist.

COPERNICUS: Precisely. How can I explain that I have revealed God's design for the universe and can find no place for God in it?

GIESE: The answer lies in the mind of God. It is not for us to know what he alone can know.

COPERNICUS: If heaven does not exist, then neither does hell. Once they figure that out, it won't be long before people will think they can do anything they please, with no threat of punishment and no promise of reward.

RHETICUS: But that does not in any way diminish the truth of your theory.

GIESE: Rheticus is right, my friend. If God devised the universe in such a manner, we must not pretend that he created it in another manner. You must publish your theory.

COPERNICUS: Can you not see what I am saying?

GIESE: Only that you are fearful of disturbing people in their comfort.

COPERNICUS: Rheticus—think about the fixed stars.

RHETICUS: They remain fixed and immovable.

COPERNICUS: Only because we cannot detect any movement among them.

RHETICUS: But they would have to be immeasurably far away—

COPERNICUS: They are.

GIESE: But they do remain fixed?

COPERNICUS: I think not. The stars, of which our earth is but an insignificant representative, extend forever.

GIESE: Forever?

COPERNICUS: For infinity.

GIESE: Infinity.

COPERNICUS: Without end.

GIESE: Is there no ultimate realm where God might dwell?

COPERNICUS does not answer.

GIESE: This is difficult to comprehend.

COPERNICUS: So is the idea that the earth moves.

GIESE: It can't be. If there is no end to things...

COPERNICUS: There is no beginning. Then what are we left to hold on to? I had believed that science would lead us to a knowledge of God. Now I feel that it takes us farther away from him.

RHETICUS: My teacher, I implore you: be the scientist you want me to become. Call up your courage and your stamina, and let this light of truth shine upon us.

COPERNICUS: Rheticus, for over a thousand years, we had lost the lamp of knowledge. Only now are we beginning to recover the learning of ancient Greece. The church is under attack by Lutherans. It will never tolerate a theory that further undermines its authority, indeed, that undermines its existence. If my book is published, it is certain to be suppressed. Gradually the work of other scientists will be suppressed, and within your lifetime the door of learning that has just been opened will be slammed shut.

RHETICUS: I find that hard to believe.

COPERNICUS: Believe whatever you wish. I know what I'm talking about.

RHETICUS: But you are a scientist. Your duty is to state the facts.

COPERNICUS: Would you have no sympathy for me? Would you throw me to the wolves?

RHETICUS: My teacher!

GIESE: You have given me a great deal to pray about. Immeasurable distances. Infinity. And still Christ has not come.

COPERNICUS: He has not.

GIESE: Yet you are convinced your theory is correct?

COPERNICUS: I am.

GIESE: Then you must publish it.

COPERNICUS: I cannot.

GIESE: Then it is settled. *(He is silent for a moment, as he formulates a strategy.)* Rheticus, I suppose you will want to return to Wittenberg at once.

RHETICUS: At once? Why?

GIESE: To resume your teaching. There is no point in staying here.

RHETICUS: We mustn't give up yet. I'm sure my teacher will endure more persuasion.

GIESE: Why torment him? He has made up his mind, and we will leave him in peace.

RHETICUS: I don't want to go back to Wittenberg.

GIESE: But you must. It was my great pleasure to meet you. I will have my man get a horse ready for you—

RHETICUS: Your Excellency—

COPERNICUS: Now, just wait. There's no need for him to rush off. There's a great deal we must talk about.

GIESE: You and I can talk later. Rheticus need not waste his time in futile discussion.

COPERNICUS: I want him to stay.

GIESE: Unless you agree to publish there is no reason for him to stay. Professor Rheticus has obligations to his university; he has students awaiting their exam results. He did not come here simply for your amusement.

Another silence.

COPERNICUS: Maybe there is a way I could publish.

GIESE: Really? What do you have in mind?

COPERNICUS: If it could be done so that my name would not appear on it...

GIESE: You want to publish anonymously? That's hardly possible.

COPERNICUS: Suppose someone were to write a short treatise summarizing my theory. To be read only by scientists. If the response were favorable, then perhaps there might be a second treatise, with more detail.

RHETICUS: This unknown summarizer would certainly acknowledge that the theory is yours.

COPERNICUS: No. My name must not appear on it.

GIESE: That would be plagiarism. No one would agree to write such an account.

COPERNICUS: Not plagiarism—perhaps the introduction could make reference to a certain Polish astronomer whose work this is...but my name must not appear.

GIESE: Why must you be so secretive? This subterfuge is not becoming in you, Nicolas. It's not at all a sensible plan.

COPERNICUS: I think it is a very sensible plan.

GIESE: Who could do it? It would have to be someone who knows your theory, and you have shown it only to Rheticus.

COPERNICUS and GIESE turn and look at RHETICUS. RHETICUS steps downstage and addresses audience.

RHETICUS: Thus was born the *Narratio Prima*, the *First Account of the Book of Revolutions*. My name appeared as the author, and I credited the work to "Doctor Nicolas of Thorn." I must confess this maneuver caused me to see my teacher as a crafty old fellow. He would remain untouched while I was sent out as target for the wrath of church, state, and common people. But I would have done anything for my teacher, and this seemed the only way to bring his theory to light. *The First Account* took me ten weeks to write, and I closed it with this hope: "May truth prevail, may daring be rewarded, may every good worker bring to light useful things in his own art, and may he search in such a manner that he appears to have sought the truth."

And where was the nearest publishing house? In Danzig. The thought of traveling to Danzig in January did not thrill me, but snow and ice cannot stop the progress of science! So off I went.

Scene Eleven

RHETICUS in Danzig. He visits ANNA in her home.

ANNA: I hear you have been quite a success here in Danzig.

RHETICUS: Everyone has been most hospitable. Mayor Ferber welcomed me warmly. Surely the gods of prosperity and generosity have smiled on the people of Prussia.

ANNA: Why are you here?

RHETICUS: For the book, of course.

ANNA: You have written a book?

RHETICUS: Not I. I have simply written a small summary. It's Dr. Copernicus's book. *The Book of Revolutions.*

ANNA: He has written a book?

RHETICUS: A magnificent book! It has been his whole life. But he would have let it perish into darkness. Fortunately, Bishop Giese persuaded him to let me write this little description. If all goes well, we hope to convince my teacher to publish the entire work.

ANNA: I doubt Giese had much to do with it. So why did you want to see me?

RHETICUS: First, let me thank you for agreeing to this visit. I know that a stranger from a strange land is not always welcome. And I am not unaware of your tenure in Frauenberg.

ANNA (offended): My tenure!

RHETICUS: I'm sorry—I don't always have the right word.

ANNA: Why don't you try "kept woman"? Or perhaps "concubine"?

RHETICUS: Madame, I beg you.

ANNA: You needn't beg. What is it that you want?

RHETICUS: I can see that your feelings are still quite strong.

ANNA: What do you want?

RHETICUS: I propose to write a biography of Dr. Copernicus—

ANNA: Nicolas?

RHETICUS: The story of his life.

ANNA: Whatever for?

RHETICUS: He is a man beyond praise, the greatest genius of our age.

ANNA: He might be a genius, but he is not a great man.

RHETICUS: Perhaps not to someone who saw him on a daily basis, but I can assure you he is a hero.

ANNA: Dr. Copernicus is a coward. He is spineless. He does not care for the people who love him. Yes, he is a good doctor, and yes, he can ably manage the affairs of Warmia, and yes, he reads a lot of books. But when it comes to what really matters in life, he is a cold man.

RHETICUS: I am not unaware that you were required to leave the cathedral.

ANNA: Eight years. I took care of him. I gave him a life.

RHETICUS: For that, I am sure he is most grateful.

ANNA: Don't be so sure. And don't expect anything from him. I hope you're not expecting anything?

RHETICUS: No. Why should I?

ANNA: Dr. Rheticus, I have never been one to hold my tongue. I see you as you are. You're a boy who is wandering this earth, looking for something—something or someone who will save you. I don't know what it might be, but I can see it in you.

RHETICUS: I don't know quite how to respond to that.

ANNA: Are you fond of Copernicus?

RHETICUS: More than fond. He is like a father to me.

ANNA: Then more's the pity. He will disappoint you.

RHETICUS: I think not.

ANNA: Trust me. You cannot count on him. He has no heart.

RHETICUS: Then—I am warned. Still, it is my intention to write the life story of my teacher. I hope you will help me. If he has no heart, I would like to hear more of it.

ANNA: And you want me to talk to you?

RHETICUS: If you will. Frau Schilling, I did not displace you. I am merely a student of the stars. I am sure that my teacher holds a special place in his heart for you.

ANNA: Has he ever mentioned me to you?

RHETICUS: No, he hasn't.

ANNA: And why should he? I am not a professor, not a mathematician. I am a mere woman. Is he well now?

RHETICUS: He seems to be.

ANNA: And who cooks for him?

RHETICUS: Karl.

ANNA: Karl! He's worthless. Who darns his socks?

RHETICUS: I couldn't say.

ANNA: Is he happy with you?

RHETICUS: I'm not sure. I think I provoke him.

ANNA (amused): Well, he could use some provoking. I envy you, Dr. Rheticus. You have something I lack—a knowledge of whatever it is that matters to him. I never really knew what he was up to. Do you?

RHETICUS: Yes. He has devised a new system. Simply put, the sun is the center of the universe, and the earth and all the planets revolve around the sun.

ANNA: Well, good luck to him. I don't think that idea will get very far.

RHETICUS: Will you tell me about his life? How he grew up, the people he knew, what he enjoys, what he detests.

ANNA (thinking): I really don't know. I looked after him. I made him comfortable. He never talked about himself.

RHETICUS: Nothing at all?

ANNA: I think not.

RHETICUS: Thank you for receiving me. I am most grateful. Please know that I am in your debt and look forward to the day when I may be of service to you.

ANNA: Oh, please! Be gone, young man.

RHETICUS: Yes, of course.

ANNA exits. RHETICUS address audience.

RHETICUS: Well! *La Schilling* was not much help, but I proceeded to soldier on with the story of my teacher's life. Slim pickings indeed...

The *Narratio Prima* was published in Danzig and became the talk of Europe—at least of learned Europe. Every astronomer from Salamanca to Vilnius wanted to know more about this theory.

Of course, there was a price to pay. I could no longer count on being the fair-haired boy of the Reformation. And once again I had to juggle my teaching duties with the truly important work of my life. One can usually find a way.

Scene Twelve

MELANCHTHON *in his study in Wittenberg.* RHETICUS, *with parted hair, enters, whistling "A Mighty Fortress is Our God."*

MELANCHTHON: This little publication of yours has certainly thrown the fat in the fire. Of course, we all know the identity of this Polish astronomer.

RHETICUS: Of course.

MELANCHTHON: What have you done to your hair?

RHETICUS: Parted it. Looks good this way, doesn't it?

MELANCHTHON: It looks decadent. *(He is amused and musses* RHETICUS'S *hair with affection.)* Don't stray too far, Rheticus. The woods are filled with the bones of those who adored new fashions, including new fashions in cosmology.

RHETICUS: You will love his theory when it is published.

MELANCHTHON: I doubt that. Joshua commanded the sun to stand still, not the earth. I am not one to correct Scripture.

RHETICUS: Copernicus is right.

MELANCHTHON: He is a fool who goes against holy writ.

RHETICUS: Then I am also a fool.

MELANCHTHON: I hope not.

RHETICUS: I suppose I must keep teaching the students at Wittenberg old lies about the heavens instead of new truths.

MELANCHTHON: They will learn about the heavens as they are laid out by God.

RHETICUS: Does Dr. Luther insist on it?

MELANCHTHON: Luther and I both insist on it.

RHETICUS: As you wish.

MELANCHTHON: Thank you.

RHETICUS: I must ask for another leave of absence.

MELANCHTHON: To continue working with that heretic?

RHETICUS: Yes.

MELANCHTHON: I cannot grant it. You said you would be in Poland for only four weeks, and you stayed three months. It is indecent of you to assert that theory in public. Think how it could disrupt society. The common people can't reason. An idea in their minds becomes a sword in their hands.

RHETICUS: The theory concerns astronomical truth, not common people and not society.

MELANCHTHON: You can't separate them. It is naive to think the scientist can speculate on the heavens and not affect the farmer at his plow.

RHETICUS: But this theory will correct many errors in our astronomy.

MELANCHTHON: It's not only the theory that disturbs me. I worry about you. I see you drifting away from Wittenberg, from the beliefs of our Lutheran faith, from the close ties we once shared.

RHETICUS: I don't feel I've drifted away.

MELANCHTHON: But what will you become? Who are astronomers and mathematicians? Cranky and lonely men, cut off from human intercourse, absorbed in their figures and charts. I don't want you to become one of them.

RHETICUS: What do you want me to become?

MELANCHTHON: A good Christian, a teacher, a husband, and a father.

RHETICUS: Marriage does not appeal to me.

MELANCHTHON: Marriage is a holy estate, an essential condition for human happiness.

RHETICUS: I'm sure married people will be glad to hear that.

MELANCHTHON: But this folly of yours—taking up with this ungodly theory, neglecting your teaching duties here, courting disgrace—

RHETICUS: I don't know what you mean.

MELANCHTHON: You know what I mean. Stay away from boys, Rheticus. Rumors fly about this continent like wildfire. Of course, we ignore them, but don't put us in the position of having to deal with fact instead of rumor.

RHETICUS: A rumor means nothing.

MELANCHTHON: It is for your own good that I speak so frankly. You are young, full of the vitality which is God's gift to youth. There is a purpose in this gift. The time has come for you to marry. You're not the first young man who has yielded to his lustful needs. In marriage, sanctified by God, family, and community, you will find the stability and gratification you need. Do you understand me?

RHETICUS: I understand. About extending my leave…

MELANCHTHON: You would still consider a leave?

RHETICUS: I must. There is so much work to be done.

MELANCHTHON: Stop and think. You are setting your life on a course that will lead to great unhappiness. There is still time for you to withdraw from this unholy obsession. There is still a place for you in the Lutheran faith.

RHETICUS: In matters of faith I remain unchanged. Why should that require me to close my mind to the truth?

MELANCHTHON: You believe this Polish astronomer is telling us the truth?

RHETICUS: I don't simply believe it. I know it.

MELANCHTHON: Then we have lost you.

RHETICUS: Does that mean I can go to Poland?

MELANCHTHON: You can go wherever you wish.

Scene Thirteen

RHETICUS and COPERNICUS in the study in Frauenberg. The year is 1540.

COPERNICUS: What do they think?

RHETICUS: Everyone says you must publish.

COPERNICUS: Did they call me a fool and a heretic?

RHETICUS: No one called you a fool. Every astronomer I talked with showed only the greatest respect and curiosity. Schoner himself called it a marvel.

COPERNICUS: I still do not wish to publish.

RHETICUS: Do you really have a choice now? If you don't publish, you will become the laughingstock of the scientific world—the famous Dr. Nicolas of Thorn who proclaimed a new universe but was afraid to tell us about it.

COPERNICUS: You were going to write a second account. That was our plan.

RHETICUS: No one wants a second account. They want your book.

COPERNICUS: It appears you have prevailed.

RHETICUS: I thought you would be pleased. Your book will place you among the immortals of history. You will rank with Aristotle and Pythagoras.

COPERNICUS: I don't want to rank with anyone.

RHETICUS: What will you do?

COPERNICUS: What can I do? I'll publish the accursed thing. As you make clear, I have no choice. There is an enormous amount of work to be done. The proofs are far from finished.

RHETICUS: Then we'll simply work them out. I'm ready.

COPERNICUS: Simply! What have I been searching for these past thirty years? You'll 'simply' find them!

RHETICUS: With work.

COPERNICUS: All right, my friend. We will find the proofs. And then we will publish—but not without the proofs.

RHETICUS: Agreed.

COPERNICUS: You don't know what's in store for you.

Scene Fourteen

RHETICUS *(to audience):* I am accustomed to the hard work of mathematics. Angles, algorithms, and cosines are like mother's milk to me. But much of the work of revolution is not merely finding the mathematical proofs. You also have to work the system. To proclaim the death of the universe as we know it requires at least three things: personal courage, support from the seats of power, and a really good publisher. Now for the first, I believe my teacher possessed an internal courage—the courage of the thinker and seeker. But he lacked...brazen audacity, shall we say, so I most humbly offered myself as the voice and face of his theory. As for the support of the powerful: the Vatican welcomed my teacher's theory. There would be no problem with Rome. Wittenberg was another story. Martin Luther had condemned the theory as heresy, and Dr Melanchthon dismissed it as merely a fiction. Further complicating matters, the really good publishing houses were all in Lutheran territory.

It would take a short history lesson to convey just how I got around their objections; let us simply say that I persuaded a certain important person—Duke Albrecht of Prussia—to placate Luther. The political battle was won, and we got the best publisher in Nuremberg.

Now the really hard work began: the task of wringing from numbers, from conjecture and imagination, from heavenly observations, from hope and terror, a real, uncorrupted picture of the universe as God created it.

RHETICUS moves to the study in Frauenberg. Discordant sound and light effects accompany his deteriorating mental state.

The intractable problem for my teacher has been the orbit of Mars, that cranky god of war. Rather like my teacher, Mars would not reveal its secret. Even with the elegant design of the sun-centered universe, Mars insisted on moving erratically. I was determined to solve the riddle with my meager tools, mathematics, patience, and the will to overcome any obstacle. I lived at my desk. Every day I would try once again to see something that remained hidden; I would try to tease out the secrets.

My teacher stopped talking to me. Mars refused to submit to his theory, and he blamed me. The numbers began to mock me. The walls closed in on me. The god Mars in full battle gear attacked me. Giant creatures chased me, howling, growling, the blood of war dripping from their skin, and evil voices shrieked in my head to give up, give up, give up.

Scene Fifteen

COPERNICUS sits at desk in study. DANTISCUS appears in doorway.

DANTISCUS: How is Dr. Rheticus doing?

COPERNICUS: He is still unconscious.

DANTISCUS: I wrote to Dr. Melanchthon to inform him.

COPERNICUS: What did you tell him?

DANTISCUS: That Rheticus had been seized, perhaps by some unruly spirit, and flung his head against the wall. And that he has remained unconscious.

COPERNICUS: What else did you tell him?

DANTISCUS: Nothing else. He wrote back and said that this has happened before. Rheticus once lost his mind. It was several weeks before he became himself again. Will he recover?

COPERNICUS: I believe he will return to health.

DANTISCUS: Let me know if there is anything I can do to help.

COPERNICUS: Thank you.

COPERNICUS goes into RHETICUS'S room. RHETICUS lies on bed unconscious. COPERNICUS sits down beside him, takes his pulse, and feels his forehead.

COPERNICUS: Rheticus, my boy. I think daily of something Thomas Aquinas wrote: "Life is so short. Our useless occupations make us numb and indifferent; and again and again swift oblivion, which embezzles our knowledge and destroys our memory, shakes out of our minds everything we knew."

If I am reluctant to fight this battle, it is because I know it is in vain. But I am grateful for what you have done. I know you paid a price, my boy. All I can do is offer you my thanks and ask your forgiveness.

COPERNICUS remains seated for a moment then exits. KARL enters with broom and starts to sweep. RHETICUS begins to stir.

KARL: You're awake! I'll get the doctor.

KARL exits. COPERNICUS enters.

RHETICUS: Where am I?

COPERNICUS: Planet Earth. Are you all right?

RHETICUS raises himself up.

RHETICUS: I think so.

COPERNICUS: Drink some water. (COPERNICUS *gives him water, which* RHETICUS *drinks.*)

RHETICUS: How long was I gone?

COPERNICUS: Three days.

RHETICUS: That's not so bad. Are we still doing the book?

COPERNICUS: Yes. We'll work. We'll work at a very steady pace, and if we don't solve the problems... Well, we will have done what we could. *(They gaze at each other.)* I missed you.

RHETICUS: Good.

Scene Sixteen

RHETICUS *at work in the study, a few months later.* KARL *enters. The year is 1541.*

KARL: May I come in?

RHETICUS: Hello, Karl.

KARL: You've kept yourself a stranger lately.

RHETICUS: The book takes all my time.

KARL: It's been months now. Do you really work all the time?

RHETICUS: Most of it. It's been dull and steady and sometimes boring, but I love it. I love the book. I love working with Dr. Copernicus.

KARL: You seem different now.

RHETICUS: It's possible. I've been thinking over some advice Dr. Melanchthon gave me. I'm beginning to know what I want.

KARL: And what is that?

RHETICUS: Work I can be proud of. A familiar face to come home to. A wife, a home, a family.

KARL: You want to marry a woman?

RHETICUS: Dr. Melanchthon has advised me to do that.

KARL: You don't sound very excited about the prospect.

RHETICUS: I think it might be the wisest course to follow.

KARL: You'd just be saving appearances.

RHETICUS: You don't approve?

KARL: A wife and a family for you would be like epicycles—they'd hide the reality. You'd become one of those eccentric planets.

RHETICUS: What an astronomer you've become!

KARL: I came here to tell you I'm leaving.

RHETICUS: Leaving? Why?

KARL: Dr. Copernicus is getting a lot weaker. When he dies, I'll be out on the street. And besides, I want to see some more of the world.

RHETICUS: Where are you going?

KARL: Nuremberg. Maybe even Italy. There's supposed to be a lot happening there. Why don't you come with me?

RHETICUS: My work is here. I can't leave now.

KARL: Work isn't everything.

RHETICUS: I can't go away with you.

KARL: I'm going to learn to read. I want to be educated.

RHETICUS: Excellent. I think you'll do well.

KARL: I liked you from the start.

RHETICUS: And I like you.

KARL: Maybe we'll meet again somewhere.

RHETICUS: Maybe. We'll see. Good-bye, Karl. Have a good journey.

KARL *exits.*

Scene Seventeen

Later that night. RHETICUS *sits on bed, fills a pipe with tobacco, lights it, and smokes. Presently* COPERNICUS *enters.*

COPERNICUS: Do you smell something burning?

RHETICUS: Yes. It is called tobacco.

COPERNICUS: You have tobacco? From the new world?

RHETICUS: Yes. I may well be the first man who has smoked in Poland. Would you like to try it? (COPERNICUS *looks doubtful.*) It has medicinal qualities.

COPERNICUS: Where did you get it?

RHETICUS: From a sailor in Danzig. He had been to America. He said it is wonderful there. Florida, they call it. White sand beaches and friendly Indians and an endless supply of tobacco.

COPERNICUS: Who was this sailor?

RHETICUS: Just some sailor.

    COPERNICUS *picks up the sack of tobacco and sniffs it.*

COPERNICUS: What is it like?

RHETICUS: It is divine.

COPERNICUS: You say it has medicinal qualities?

RHETICUS: It soothes the nerves, cleanses the blood, and induces a feeling of euphoria. Go ahead and try it.

COPERNICUS: It's unchristian.

RHETICUS: Most vices are.

COPERNICUS: What will happen if I do?

RHETICUS: Nothing. I won't tell a soul.

COPERNICUS takes a puff, then a second, then a third.

COPERNICUS: I can detect medicinal qualities.

RHETICUS: I thought you might.

COPERNICUS: Could this take your mind off the stars?

RHETICUS: I suppose it could, if you smoked enough.

COPERNICUS: You seem melancholy tonight.

RHETICUS: Sometimes I think there's no place for me. Nobody really wants me.

COPERNICUS: That's not true. You've been very favorably received. Everyone finds you gracious and delightful.

RHETICUS: Yes, I do have this beguiling presence. But beyond that, I don't have a resting place where I can stop worrying about being clever and pleasant and just be Rheticus.

COPERNICUS: I used to feel that way. You grow out of it. You have your work. You begin to feel not so lonely after a few years.

RHETICUS: I've been thinking about your brother.

COPERNICUS: Andreas?

RHETICUS: You're afraid I'll turn out like him, aren't you?

COPERNICUS: That thought has crossed my mind.

RHETICUS: You think I'll lead a dissolute life and die of syphilis?

COPERNICUS: I hope not, but anything is possible.

RHETICUS: Are you going to disown me?

COPERNICUS: There have been times when I was close to it.

RHETICUS: I want to take the manuscript to Nuremberg now.

COPERNICUS: We still haven't found all the proofs.

RHETICUS: Do you think we ever will? Some day, somehow, the proofs will be found. I don't think we will be the ones to do it. But you must publish the theory.

COPERNICUS: There's no need to rush.

RHETICUS: That's what you said three years ago.

COPERNICUS: It's been three years?

RHETICUS: Time moves upon us rapidly.

COPERNICUS: I'm sorry. I can't let you publish.

RHETICUS: I'll pretend you never said that.

COPERNICUS: I know you've worked hard, I know you've gotten nothing in return, but I can't let you publish my book. It will be ridiculed. I will look like a fool—and I can't bear that.

RHETICUS: I am sick to death of handling you as if you were a delicate flower. You are not so delicate. So what if somebody critcizes you? So what if you're a fool? If you're going to tinker with the structure of the universe, you'd better be ready to face the consequences.

COPERNICUS: There would be no consequences if you had never come here.

RHETICUS: And your book would go to the grave with you.

COPERNICUS: Yes.

RHETICUS: Is that what you want? To throw your life's work away? To waste your gifts?

COPERNICUS: No, that's not what I want.

RHETICUS: I didn't think so. You can be a very difficult man. I'm leaving tomorrow.

COPERNICUS: Tomorrow?

RHETICUS: Yes, tomorrow. I'm taking the manuscript to Nuremberg.

COPERNICUS: I haven't composed the dedication yet.

RHETICUS: You can send it to me in Wittenberg. I plan to stop there for a few days.

COPERNICUS: It has not been easy for me to trust you.

RHETICUS: I'm not sure that you do.

COPERNICUS: Believe me, I do. I am bound to you by the new universe, and that is a bond stronger than blood or sentiment. My legacy is not children, not my name, but my book—and I look to you to preserve it. You are my heir.

RHETICUS: Do you mean that?

COPERNICUS: Yes. You are the disciple I had hoped for. You are the son I never had.

Scene Eighteen

COPERNICUS'S *study in Frauenberg. He is propped up in bed.* GIESE *enters. The year is 1542.*

GIESE: Nicolas. It is Tiedemann. Your friend.

COPERNICUS: Yes. Thank you for coming to see an old man. I am dying. I need your help.

GIESE: Are you prepared?

COPERNICUS: To die? No. But that's not why I need you. There is still work to do on the book.

GIESE: I could try, but I'm no astronomer.

COPERNICUS: It's not that. It's the dedication. Let me dictate it to you.

GIESE: Very well. *(GIESE writes as COPERNICUS speaks.)*

COPERNICUS: "To his eminence, Pope Paul III, this book is dedicated.
"It was with great trepidation that I set out upon this enterprise, fearing the ridicule it could cause, and often

I thought of abandoning the whole project. But my misgivings and protests were overcome by my friends.

"First among these was Nicolas Schonberg, cardinal of Capua. Next to him comes my very dear friend Tiedemann Giese, bishop of Kulm, whose encouragement allowed me to present this work. Not a few other eminent and scholarly men urged me, and thus have I yielded to their persuasion, and at long last permit my friends to publish the work they have so long demanded..."

GIESE: Nicolas—haven't you forgotten someone?

COPERNICUS: No. That's everyone I wish to thank.

GIESE: Rheticus. Surely you want to acknowledge his efforts.

COPERNICUS: I want to. But I can't.

GIESE: Yes, you can. You simply say that this young mathematician inspired you to bring your book to the world.

COPERNICUS: This young heretic sodomite mathematician?

GIESE: It's not for you to sit in judgment. Our Lord will decide if Rheticus is a sinner or not.

COPERNICUS: It's not the Lord I'm concerned with, it's the pope. I want my book to be respected. There is no need to thank a Lutheran.

GIESE: It's very unkind of you.

COPERNICUS: Rheticus will understand.

GIESE: And if he doesn't?

COPERNICUS: He'll understand.

Scene Nineteen

RHETICUS and MELANCHTHON in Wittenberg.

MELANCHTHON: I didn't expect to see you, but it's just as well you're here.

RHETICUS: I am on my way to the printers in Nuremberg.

MELANCHTHON: You're publishing his theory?

RHETICUS: Yes. It still has some unresolved problems, but we cannot wait; my teacher grows weaker with each day. I would like for him to see the book in print.

MELANCHTHON: That book is no concern of mine.

RHETICUS: I need to ask for an extension of my leave from teaching duties.

MELANCHTHON: Not granted. I would like to know something. I would like to know if it is true that you committed the Italian perversion with a young servant in Frauenberg. *(RHETICUS is silent.)* The young man I speak of is now living here in Wittenberg. He established an unwholesome liaison with a man and told him you were his close friend. Word then began to spread. It is no credit to the University of Wittenberg to have a sodomite as head of its mathematics department. Do you have anything to say for yourself?

RHETICUS: Karl, I suppose.

MELANCHTHON: Karl, you suppose? Among how many others? Rheticus, I have protected you for years now. Your little scrapes and adventures left you largely unscathed because Dr. Melanchthon was there to defend you. Wild oats, I said. Be patient with the boy—the result of this insane age we're living in, where morals have disappeared and chaos rules supreme. But this is the limit. You may not receive an extension of your leave, and you may not remain on the faculty of Wittenberg.

RHETICUS: I'm sure this can be resolved amicably.

MELANCHTHON: You will probably want to apply for a position at the University of Leipzig. The dean is a friend of mine. Your application will be favorably received. Leipzig has no knowledge of any impropriety. Your reputation there will be secure, if you can keep it that way.

RHETICUS: Where is Karl now?

MELANCHTHON: In jail. He will be tried for crimes against nature. Most likely he will be hanged.

RHETICUS: He's hardly more than a boy. He's never hurt anyone.

MELANCHTHON, still angry, begins to mellow.

MELANCHTHON: I will try to have him banished.

RHETICUS: Does Dr. Copernicus know about this?

MELANCHTHON: You can be sure of it.

RHETICUS: His manuscript is still in Nuremberg. I need to be there.

MELANCHTHON: Find someone else to do the job.

RHETICUS: It's very technical. There's no one else who could do it.

MELANCHTHON: I suggest Andreas Osiander.

RHETICUS: Osiander? He's a theologian, not a mathematician.

MELANCHTHON: But he has corresponded with Copernicus, and he is a faithful Lutheran. You don't really have a choice.

RHETICUS: When do they want me in Leipzig?

MELANCHTHON: Next week. (*MELANCHTHON gives letter to RHETICUS.*) This came for you today.

RHETICUS reads the letter, then sits down, stunned and dismayed.

MELANCHTHON: What's wrong?

RHETICUS: It's my teacher's dedication.

He gives letter to MELANCHTHON, who reads it.

MELANCHTHON: It's dedicated to Pope Paul III. What did you expect?

RHETICUS: I can see the wisdom of it. The pope's good will is vital to the future of his theory. Read the rest.

MELANCHTHON: "This work could not have been done without the aid and encouragement of my friends...Nicolas Schonberg, cardinal of Capua...Tiedemann Giese, bishop of Kulm."

RHETICUS: Where is my name?

MELANCHTHON: Nowhere.

RHETICUS: Nowhere. It's as if he never knew me.

MELANCHTHON: I'm sorry. Life often disappoints us. But you must put this behind you. You have a new position in Leipzig. A chance to start over. In Leipzig no one will know what has happened. You can change your ways. You can become the respected professor, the husband and father who embodies the Lutheran faith.

RHETICUS: He didn't even mention my name.

Scene Twenty

The study in Frauenberg. ANNA *and* GIESE *attend* COPERNICUS, *who is dying.* RHETICUS *enters.*

ANNA: Rheticus. You should not have come.

RHETICUS: I want to see him.

GIESE: Your teacher is near death.

RHETICUS: So am I.

GIESE: I know why you have come. It was an unpleasant oversight that he did not mention you in the dedication.

RHETICUS: It was more than unpleasant.

GIESE: It was not indifference toward you, but inattention.

RHETICUS: It was indifference. And malice. He cares nothing for me.

GIESE: His mind has wandered; his faculties are impaired.

RHETICUS: He was rational enough to write a very clever dedication and heartless enough to leave me out of it. Why, just once in his life, couldn't he show some courage?

COPERNICUS rises.

ANNA: You mustn't.

COPERNICUS: No, leave me. Please, Anna, leave. Bishop Giese.

ANNA: I am staying here with you.

COPERNICUS: I'll be all right. Let me talk to him alone. He deserves as much.

GIESE: Come, Anna.

GIESE and ANNA exit.

RHETICUS: Why did you do it?

COPERNICUS: I knew no other way. It took all my nerve just to publish the book. I couldn't include you in it, too.

RHETICUS: Why?

COPERNICUS: Rheticus, everything about you is wrong. You're a Lutheran, you don't revere the old ways, you disregard the demands of respectable society. I couldn't risk that for my book.

RHETICUS: If it weren't for me, you wouldn't have a book. It doesn't matter if I am a heretic or slept with your servant. What matters is that I am the one person who cajoled you and humored you and loved you into printing your book of revolutions. And you dismiss me without so much as an apology.

COPERNICUS: I offer my apology.

RHETICUS: I don't want it. I want you to say you are not afraid to prove the earth moves, not afraid to publish the truth, not afraid to acknowledge me.

COPERNICUS: Forget all this. I will die soon. The book will be yours. The work will be yours to carry on. You are my disciple.

RHETICUS: No. The disciple is dead. You killed him.

COPERNICUS: I see. There will be others.

RHETICUS: Yes. There will be others.

> RHETICUS *bursts into tears, falls to his knees before* COPERNICUS, *who cautiously strokes* RHETICUS'S *head.*

RHETICUS: I loved you so much.

COPERNICUS: You shouldn't have.

> RHETICUS *regains his composure.*

RHETICUS: You called me your son. I thought you loved me.

COPERNICUS: I do.

RHETICUS: Then why? I gave you my whole life.

COPERNICUS: And I gave you mine. I gave you my book, and I have given that to no one else.

RHETICUS: But the dedication…

COPERNICUS: Judge me by my own lights, not by yours. You are filled with courage and enthusiasm. I admire that in you, but I lack those qualities. The simplest step for you is a dreaded, difficult journey for me.

RHETICUS: It doesn't have to be that way.

COPERNICUS: Maybe in this new age of yours it doesn't. What will you do now?

RHETICUS: I don't know. Go to Florida and never come back.

COPERNICUS: The new world? Come now.

RHETICUS: In America there are no astronomers who will betray you. There are no teachers who will use you and abuse you. I will lie on the white sands and smoke tobacco and forget that I ever knew Dr. Copernicus.

COPERNICUS: Dr. Copernicus will never forget that he knew you.

RHETICUS: I wish I could believe that.

COPERNICUS: Try not to be so hard on me.

RHETICUS: I wish none of this had ever happened.

COPERNICUS: I know. I wish that we never had to learn there is no comfort for us on earth. It is only for mathematicians to know.

Scene Twenty-One

RHETICUS alone on stage. Behind him, a dark blue sky filled with stars.

RHETICUS: A confession: the scene you just witnessed never happened. After I left Frauenberg with the manuscript, I never saw him again. But I wish I had. How could he betray me like that? For years I imagined a final confrontation—I would give him, at long last, the chance to be the hero I wanted him to be. A chance to champion the truth, not simply disclose it. A chance to tell me that I mattered to him.

My teacher died on the very day his book was published. I heard from Bishop Giese that he received a copy on his deathbed. An apocryphal story, perhaps, but it appeals to me: having gotten that child born, my teacher could be counted on to abandon it.

The book did not cause the slightest ripple among clergy or laity. This was because Andreas Osiander, after my forced removal to Leipzig, inserted a false preface. He said the theory was not intended to be true but was simply a new way of calculating the movements of the stars, a useful tool for navigators and so forth.

In time I got chased out of Leipzig—boy trouble again—and went to Italy, where I pursued the study of medicine. Word got round back in Germany that I had become unhinged, gone a little crazy, and died. Another false preface. I never married, of course; I may have broken the rules, but I was never dishonest.

Many years passed and I grew old, my heart empty, my good name in ruins, my mind barely within the realms of reason—Rheticus thought by friend and foe alike to be a wreck. I had hung onto the manuscript of my teacher's biography, surely a book that would give me a place in history. But somehow it disappeared amidst my comings and goings. Finally, I landed in Krakow, where I built obelisks and wrote the most amazing almanacs. I gained much renown for my astrological skills. Then, one day—and this is true—I heard a knock at my door. I opened, and there stood young Valentine Otho, a student from the University of Wittenberg. He had heard of my work with my beloved triangles and wanted to study with me. How my heart leapt! Could life really be so kind to me? "Young Otho," I said, "you are exactly the same age as I when I sought my teacher in Poland." How I relived those days by the Baltic shore, those long nights when we looked upon the stars and God's grand design was revealed to us. How I missed my teacher! I had learned so much; now I could forgive so much. And bless young Otho! He brought back a joy in learning I had all but forgotten, and he knew nothing of its pain. These are memories that swift oblivion will not erase. Then let us take heart: truth will prevail, daring will be rewarded, we may all bring to light useful things in our chosen art—if we have sought the truth.

End.

NOTES AND COMMENTS

About Rheticus

Georg Joachim Iserin was born in Feldkirch, Austria, on February 16, 1514. His father, Philip Iserin, practiced medicine and was apparently well established in the town. Thomasina de Porris, wife of Iserin and mother of Rheticus, descended from an Italian family said to be wealthy. When Rheticus was fourteen, his father was convicted of embezzlement. Despite Thomasina's efforts to secure his release, Iserin was beheaded in Feldkirch. According to custom, the family could no longer use the Iserin name and assumed Thomasina's name, translated into German. Rheticus thus became Georg Joachim von Lauchen. In keeping with the humanist Renaissance fashion, he adopted the latinized name of Rheticus, indicating his origin in the ancient Roman province of Rhaetia.

Rheticus was sent to the Fraumünster school in Zurich, where he remained for four years. At age eighteen, he enrolled at the University of Wittenberg and flourished there under the guidance of Philipp Melanchthon. After earning his master's degree, he was appointed professor of "lower mathematics." Rheticus very early exhibited a keen desire to increase his knowledge of mathematics, astronomy, and astrology; in pursuit of such knowledge he presented himself to various scholars throughout Germany. He heard of the rumored heliocentric theory, developed by the obscure Copernicus, and in 1539 set off to find the man and his theory. He stayed with Copernicus for over two years and convinced him to publish *De Revolutionibus*, a new model of the universe.

His subsequent achievements in life were never so spectacular, though he made valuable contributions to mathematics. In 1542 he assumed a teaching position at Leipzig;

this move is puzzling as it required him to give up the task of overseeing the publication of *De Revolutionibus*, a book that he passionately cared about.

Life in Leipzig began relatively smoothly despite his apparent restlessness. Disaster struck in 1551 when the father of a student accused Rheticus of getting his son drunk and sodomizing him. Rheticus immediately fled Leipzig, going to Prague and enrolling in medical school. After a prolonged trial, Rheticus was found guilty *in absentia* and banished from Leipzig for 101 years.

The itinerant years followed, with travels to Italy and periods of ill health and recovery at his mother's home (she was by then married to the mayor of Bregenz). He settled in Krakow in 1554, where he remained for eighteen years. During this time, he practiced medicine, supplemented his income by writing almanacs and horoscopes, and hired six assistants to work on his trigonometric tables. This enormous work, published after his death as *Opus Palatinum de triangulis*, laid the basis for modern trigonometry. He left Krakow in 1572 for Cassovia (now Kosice, Slovakia). The unexpected arrival of Valentine Otho in 1574 must have brought a moment of happiness to Rheticus. He died a few months later, and Otho took up the unfinished work on the tables. This work remained a useful reference tool for mathematicians until the early twentieth century.

For further reading: The only full-length English-language biography of Rheticus is *The First Copernican* (2006), an excellent account by Dennis Danielson. *The Sleepwalkers* (1959), Arthur Koestler's survey of astronomy from Pythagoras to Newton, includes a compelling account of Rheticus and Copernicus. For readers in German, the standard biography is *Georg Joachim Rhetikus* (1967), by Karl Heinz Burmeister.

About the Cover

No portrait of Rheticus has been found, although one was painted during his lifetime. Lacking an image of Rheticus, I elected to go with a portrait of another young man of the same period, Derich Born (1510-1549), painted by Hans Holbein the Younger. Born was a twenty-three-year-old Hanseatic merchant at the London Steelyard when he sat for Holbein. The portrait is now part of the Queen's Gallery collection in London.

Place Names

The geopolitical history of the southeastern Baltic coast—an area that we know today as Poland—is complicated. In *Eccentric Planet* I have chosen to use the names of towns as they were known in the 16th century, the period in which the action occurs. For the region where Copernicus lived I use the modern designation, which is Poland. It was called Ermland, by the Germans, and Warmia, by the Poles. I make the assumption that most contemporary readers will have no idea where Warmia or Ermland might fit on a map, hence the designation as Poland.

About This Play

In **The Sleepwalkers** (1959), Arthur Koestler introduces Rheticus as:

> ...*one of the knights errant of the Renaissance whose enthusiasm fanned borrowed sparks into flame...an* enfant terrible, *an inspired fool, a* condottiere *of science, an adoring disciple and, fortunately, either homo- or bi-sexual after the fashion of the time. I say "fortunately" because the so afflicted have always proved to be the most devoted teachers and disciples, from Socrates to this day, and History owes them a debt.*

This was my first encounter with Rheticus, and I was captivated. The year was 1971. Koestler's engaging, almost novelistic style made for easy reading, a great help since I was neither a scientist nor a mathematician. I was, however, a young gay man in Georgia struggling to come to terms with this basic fact of my life. Despite the "so afflicted," this was the first time I'd seen anyone have a good word to say about homosexuals. Koestler's remarks were all the more remarkable, coming as they did in 1959. (Of course, if Koestler had described Rheticus as "unfortunately" homosexual, I might never have written this play.) Subsequently, I read as much about him as I could find, which in the 1970s—in English—was not very much. By 1980 I felt ready to create my version of Rheticus's encounter with Copernicus. While staying for a month at the William Flanagan Center in Montauk, New York, I wrote the first draft of *Eccentric Planet*.

The next year I visited Feldkirch, Austria, where Rheticus was born, and met Dr. Karl Heinz Burmeister, whose biography of Rheticus remains definitive. In 1982 this play was awarded a CAPS playwriting grant by the New York State Council on the Arts and was produced at Trinity Theater, New York, in 1983.

In the years that I have worked on this play, through readings and production and frequent revision, I have never ceased to find Rheticus an intriguing and lovable figure. It is my hope that *Eccentric Planet* will shed more light on this remarkable man. His closing words to the *Narratio Prima* are worth repeating here:

> *May truth prevail, may daring be rewarded, may every good worker bring to light useful things in his own art, and may he search in such a manner that he appears to have sought the truth.*

Eccentric Planet is available in German.
For more information, please contact:
    Bochert Translations
    Kiefholzstrasse 1 [K1]
    12435 Berlin
    Deutschland
    www.bochert.com

www.ingramcontent.com/pod-product-compliance
Lightning Source LLC
Chambersburg PA
CBHW031404040426
42444CB00005B/418